Saint Peter's Pearly Gates

By
Clarke Smith

Cadmus Publishing
www.cadmuspublishing.com

Copyright © 2022 Clarke Smith

Published by Cadmus Publishing
www.cadmuspublishing.com
Port Angeles, WA

ISBN: 978-1-63751-152-7
LCCN: 2022901781

All rights reserved. Copyright under Berne Copyright Convention, Universal Copyright Convention, and Pan-American Copyright Convention. No part of this book may be reproduced, stored in a retrieval system, or transmitted in any form, or by any means, electronic, mechanical, photocopying, recording or otherwise, without prior permission of the author.

Acknowledgements

This book could not have been written without my good friend and Father, Jesus, and prayer from the Apostolic Church Brothers and Sisters. I am also very deeply grateful to Bonnieview Keyser Church. Special thanks go to Pastor Richard Cavey, my Pastor and true Brother in Christ Jesus, who taught the Apostolic faith. Also, my Brother D.J. Smith continues to be a source of strength and support, his kindness, rooted deeply, is an inspiration to me, always there for me.

I dedicate this book to all those who truly seek the Kingdom of Heaven.

Contents

Introduction 1

Chapter 1 Who Is Jesus? 3

Quiz - Who Is Jesus? 7

Go Tell It on the Mountain 8

Chapter 2 - Who is Apostle Peter? 10

I've Got the Keys to the Kingdom Song 13

Chapter 3 - What Is Faith? 15

Chapter 3 Song - Psalm 150:1-6 18

Chapter 4 - What is the Cornerstone? 19

What A Mighty God We Serve Song 22

Chapter 5 - How Do you Know You're Saved? 24

Chapter 6 - Where Are the Dead? 31

Questions – True or False 39

Prayer for Pardon 41

Chapter 7- True Christmas Story 43

Chapter 8 - Who Will Feed My Sheep? 45

Chapter 9 - The Serpent or Sin 48

Chapter 10 - The Bible 54

Chapter 10 Questions – Yes or No 59

Final Warning 61

Chapter 11 66

Walking In the Kingdom 68

Conclusion 76

INTRODUCTION

I'm a born-again Christian, just like Apostle Paul, who wrote most of the books in the New Testament, written in prison. Once we are saved by the Holy Ghost's gift, we reach out to help save the lost, for the Kingdom of Heaven. Everyone has heard the saying, "I'll soon go to Saint Peter's pearly gates," or the upper room, both are used a lot.

So many people often forget that Jesus gave Apostle Peter the keys to the Kingdom. In Matthew 16:16-19 Bind on Earth and He bound on Earth shall be bound in Heaven. Jesus's words to Peter.

Those first apostles in the early first church, open the keys and gates, for us all, them and all afar off. They were working for Jesus, I'm working for Jesus, in these afar off days, trying to help all into Saint Peter's pearly gates. I believe eternal life is too important to almost make Heaven. As I slowly show all, the only way to Heaven's gates, please share the book with family, Brothers or Sisters, or friends.

Saint Peter was converted, Jesus told Peter, when thou are converted, strengthen thou Brothers. Luke 22:29-32 When now let us start this book into action, going towards those gates.

CLARKE SMITH

Chapter 1 Who Is Jesus?

OT = Old Testament
NT = New Testament
OT
Genesis 1:1-31 God created everything and saw it was good.
NT
John 1:10 He was in the world, and the world was made by him and the world knew him not.
OT
Job 9:8 Which alone spreadeth out the heavens, and treadest upon the waves of the sea.
NT
John 10:30 I and my Father are one; Verse 33, Maketh thyself God.
Matthew 14:26,27 Verse 26 And when the disciples saw him walk on the sea,
OT
Psalm 104:3 Who layeth the beams of his chambers in the water who walketh upon the clouds as his chariot.

NT

Acts 1:9 And when he had spoken these things, while they beheld he was taken up; and a cloud received him out of their sight.

OT

Isaiah 9:6 The mighty God, the everlasting Father

37:16 O Lord of hosts, God of Israel, that dwellest between the cherubims, thou art the God, even thou alone, of all the Kingdom of the Earth, thou has made Heaven and Earth.

Isaiah 45:18 For this saith the Lord that created the Heavens, God himself that formed the Earth and made it, he hath established it, he created it not in vain, he formed it to be inhabited, I am the Lord, and there is none else.

Daniel 7:9 Ancient of days did set, whose garment was white as snow and the hair of his head like pure wool; his throne like fiery flames.

NT

Revelation 1:12-18 Verse 14 His head and his hairs were white like wool, as white as snow; his eyes were as a flame of fire; Verse 17, And when I saw him, I fell at his feet as dead, and he laid his right hand upon me, saying unto me, fear not; I am the first and the last; Verse 18 I am he that liveth, and was dead; and have the keys of Hell and of Death.

OT

Deuteronomy 6:4 Hear, O Israel; the Lord our God is one Lord.

32:39 See now that I, even I am he, and there is no God with me; I kill, and I make alive; I wound, and I heal, neither is there any that can deliver out of my hand.

OT

II Samuel 2:6 The Lord killeth, and maketh alive, he bringeth down to the grave, and bringeth up.

Nehemiah 9:6 Thou, even thou, art Lord alone; thou hast made Heaven the heaven of heavens, with all the host, the earth, and all things that are there in, the seas, and all there in.

Psalm 86:10 For thou art great, and wondrous things, thou art God alone

Psalm 124:8 Our help is in the name of the Lord, who made Heaven and Earth.

NT

John 10:30 I and my Father are one.

11:25 Jesus said unto her, I am the resurrection, and the life.

8:56,57,58 Verse 56 Your father Abraham rejoiced to see my day; and saw it and was glad. Verse 57, 58 Jesus said unto them, verily, verily, I say unto you, before Abraham was I am.

OT

17:1 And when Abram was ninety years old and nine, the Lord appeared to Abram, and said unto him, I am the Almighty God, walk before me, and be thou perfect.

18:1-33 Verse 1 And the Lord appeared unto him in the plains of Mamre and he sat in the tent door in the heat of the day.

Psalm 124:8 Our help is in the name of the Lord, who made Heaven and Earth.

Zechariah 14:1-12 Verse 5 And the Lord my God shall come, and all the saints with thee; Verse 9 And the Lord shall be king over all the Earth; in that day shall there be one Lord, and his name one.

Malachi 1:11 For from the rising of the sun even unto the going down of the same my name shall be great among the Gentiles.

NT

Matthew 28:18 And Jesus came and spoke unto them, saying, all power is given unto me in Heaven and in Earth.

Mark 2:10 But that ye may know that the Son of man has power on Earth to forgive sins (he saith to the palsy); Verse 11 Arise

Mark 12:29 And Jesus answered him, the first of all the commandments is, Hear, O Israel; the Lord our God is one Lord.

John 5:43 I am come in my Father's name, and ye receive me not; if another shall come in (his own name) him ye will receive.

John 10:30 I and my Father are one; 12:45 And he that seeth me seeth him that sent me; 14:6 Jesus saith unto him, I am the way; the truth, and the life; no man cometh unto the Father, but by me; Verse 7 If ye known me, you should have known my Father also; and from henceforth ye know him, and have seen him; Verse 15 If ye love me, keep my commandments.

Acts 20:28 Take heed therefore unto yourselves, and to all the flock over which the Holy Ghost has made you overseers, to feed the church of God, which he hath purchased with his blood.

I John 3:16 Hereby perceive we the love of God.

Quiz - Who Is Jesus?

1. A. Questions Who is the Father?
B. Answers-Yours
2. A. Questions Who is the Son?
B. Answers-Yours
3. A. Questions Who is the Holy Ghost?
B. Answers-Yours
4. A. Questions Who will be in you?
B. Answers-Yours
5. A. Questions Who will judge us all?
B. Answers-Yours

Go Tell It on the Mountain

Misc. Christmas

```
D                       A               D-
Go tell it on the mountain, over the hills and everywhere;
D                         A7             D
Go tell it on the mountain that Jesus Christ is born.
         D                          A             D
    While shepherds kept their watching o'er silent flocks by
night,
                              A         A7
Behold throughout the heavens there shone a Holy Light.
D                       A               D-
Go tell it on the mountain, over the hills and everywhere;
D                         A7             D
Go tell it on the mountain that Jesus Christ is born.
         D                                A           D
    The shepherds feared and trembled when lo! Above the
earth,
```

         A   A7
Rang out the angel chorus that hailed our Savior's birth.
D   A   D-
Go tell it on the mountain, over the hills and everywhere;
D   A7   D
Go tell it on the mountain that Jesus Christ is born.
   D   A   D
Down in a lowly manger the humble Christ was born
          A   A
And brought us God's salvation that blessed Christmas morn!
D   A   D-
Go tell it on the mountain, over the hills and everywhere;
D   A7   D
Go tell it on the mountain that Jesus Christ is born.

Chapter 2 - Who is Apostle Peter?

NT

Matthew 4:18 And Jesus, walking by the Sea of Galilee, saw two brethren, Simon called Peter, and Andrew his brother, cast a net into the sea: for they were fishers; Verse 19 And he saith unto them, follow me, and I will make you fishers of men; Verse 20 And they straightway left their nets, and followed him.

Matthew 10:1 And when he called unto him his twelve disciples, he gave them power against unclean spirits, to cast them out, and to heal all manner of sickness and all manner of disease.

Matthew 14:29 And he said, come, and when Peter was come down out of the ship, he walked on water, to go to Jesus; Verse 18 And I say until thee, that thou art Peter, and unto this rock I will build (my) church; and the gates of Hell shall not prevail against it; Verse 19 I will give unto thee the keys of the Kingdom of Heaven: and whatsoever thou shalt lose on Earth shall be loosed in Heaven.

Matthew 17:1 And after six days Jesus taketh Peter, James, and John his brother, and bringeth them to a high mountain apart; Verse 2 And was transfigured before them, and his face did shine as the sun, and his raiment was white as the light; Verse 3 And behold, there appeared unto them, Moses and Elias talking with him.

17:26 Peter saith unto him, of strangers, Jesus saith unto him, then are the children free; Verse 27 Notwithstanding, lest we should offend them, go to the sea, and cast a hook, and take up the fish that first cometh up; and when thou opened his mouth, thou shalt find a piece of money; that take, and give unto them for me and thee.

26:35 Peter said unto him, though I should die with thee, yet will I not deny thee. Likewise said all, so said all the disciples; Verse 72 And again he denied with an oath, I do not know the man.

NT

Luke 22:62 And Peter went out, and wept bitterly.

Luke 24:1 Now upon the first day of the week, very early in the morning, they came unto the sepulchre, the spices which they had prepared, and certain other with them; Verse 6 He is not here, but is risen; remember how he spoke this unto you when he was yet in Galilee; Verse 12 Then arose Peter, and ran unto the sepulchre; Verse 49 And, behold, I send the promise of my Father upon you: but tarry ye in the city of Jerusalem, until ye be endued with power from on high.

Acts 1:15 And in those days Peter stood up in the midst of the disciples, and said (the number of names together were about a hundred and twenty).

2:4 And they were all filled with the Holy Ghost, and began to speak in other tongues, as the Spirit gave them utterance.

Acts 9 Verse 44 While Peter yet spoke these words, the Holy Ghost fell on all them which heard the word.

First Peter An apostle of Jesus Christ, to the strangers scattered throughout Pontus, Galatia, Cappadocia, Asia, Bithynia. Peter wrote the book.

3:21 The like figure where unto even baptism doth also now save us (not the putting away of the filth of the flesh, but the answer of a good conscience towards God) by the resurrection of Jesus Christ.

II Peter 1:1 Simon Peter, a servant and an apostle of Jesus Christ, to them that have obtained like precious faith with us through the righteousness of God, and our savior Jesus Christ: Peter wrote book.

Revelation 21:14 And the wall of the city had twelve fountains, and in them the names of the twelve Apostles of the Lamb.

Apostle Peter was Jesus's gatekeeper, words of faith, to true salvation, from a fisherman to a true saint.

I've Got the Keys to the Kingdom Song

I've got the keys to the Kingdom, and this world can't do me no harm
I got the keys to the Kingdom, and this world can't do me no harm.
I know Him as the Father,
I know Him as the Son,
And I know Him as the Holy Ghost,
And I know these three are one.
I've got the keys to the Kingdom,
I've got got the keys to the Kingdom,
I got the keys to the Kingdom.

My Sister Ruth sang that song, that lovely voice was like an angel from Heaven singing. I hope and pray someday I can record a CD with her, if I can someday, I'll send it with a book, hope in due time, we can bless you with that nice song. Only God knows the future moments of our earthly time, events.

Brother Bill, always sang his lifelong song. He went on to be with the Lord, we shall sing it together again in Heaven, that day.

I FEEL LIKE TRAVELING ON, Brother Bills' favorite song, as one of our many heavenly songs.

Till we all go marching into Heaven some glad day.
Oh, what it will be, joy, peace, love, nor pain, nor death.
Just all of us Brothers and Sisters, walking with our Lord.

Chapter 3 - What Is Faith?

NT

Hebrews 11:1 Now faith is the substance of things hoped for, the evidence of things not seen.

Matthew 15:28 Then Jesus answered her and said unto her, O woman, great is thy faith, be it unto thee even as thou wilt. And her daughter was made whole from that very hour.

Hebrews 10:38 Now the just shall live by faith, but if any man draw back, my soul shall not have no pleasure in him.

11:3-35 Verse 6 But without faith it is impossible to please him; for he that cometh to God must believe that he is, and that he is a rewarder of them that diligently seek him; Verse 13 These all died in faith, not having received the promises; but having seen them afar off, and were persuaded of them, and embraced them, and confessed that they were strangers and pilgrims on Earth; Verse 30 By faith the walls of Jericho fell down, after they circled.

12:2 Looking unto Jesus the author and finisher of our faith; who for the joy that was set before him endured the cross, despising the shame, and is set down at the right hand of the Throne of God.

James 1:3 Knowing this, that the trying of your faith worketh patience.

2:5 Hearken, my beloved brethren, hath not God chosen the poor of this world rich in faith, and heirs of the Kingdom which he promised to them that love him; Verse 17 Even so faith if it has not works, is dead, being alone; Verse 18 Yea, a man may say, thou has faith and I have works; show me thy faith without thy works, and I know, o vain man, that faith without works is dead?; Verse 24 Ye see then how that by works a man is justified, and not be faith only.

Chapter 3 Verse 8 But the tongue can no man tame; it is an unruly evil, full of deadly poison.

Acts 8:13 Then Simon himself believed also; and when he was baptized, he continued with Philip, and wondered, beholding the things, miracles and signs which were done; Verse 14 Now when the apostles which were at Jerusalem heard that Samaria had received the word of God, they sent unto them Peter and John; Verse 15 Who when they come down, prayed for them, that they might received the Holy Ghost; Verse 16 (For as yet he was fallen upon none of them; only they were baptized in the name of the Lord Jesus); Verse 17 Then laid thy hands on them, and they received the Holy Ghost; Verse 18 And when Simon saw that through laying on the Apostle's hands the Holy Ghost was given, he offered them money; Verse 19 Saying, give me also this power, that on whosoever I lay hands, he may receive the Holy Ghost; Verse 20 But Peter said unto him, thy money perish with thee, because thou hast thought that the gift of God may be purchased with money.

Please take notice Simon believed and was baptized, yet he

did not receive the gift of the Holy Ghost, he seen others receive the gift.

Chapter 9:1 And Saul, yet breathing out threatenings and slaughter against the disciples of the Lord, went unto the High Priest; Verse 3 And as he journeyed, he came near Damascus; and suddenly there shined round about him a light from Heaven; Verse 6 And he trembling and astonished said, Lord, what will thou have me to do? And the Lord said until him, Arise, and go into the city, and it shall be told what thou must do; Verse 17 And Ananias went his way, and entered into the house; and putting his hands on him said, Brother Saul, the Lord, even Jesus, that appeared unto thee in the way as thou camest, hath sent me, that thou mightest receive thy sight, and be filled with the Holy Ghost; Verse 18 And immediately there fell from his eyes as it had been scales; and he received sight forthwith, and arose, and was baptized.

Philippians 2:12 Wherefore, my beloved, as ye have always obeyed, not as in my presence only, but now so much more in my absence, work out your own salvation with fear and trembling.

I Timothy 2:4 Who will have all men to be saved, and to come unto the knowledge of Truth.

II Timothy 2:15 Study to show thyself approved unto God, a work man that needeth not to be ashamed, rightly dividing the word of Truth.

Chapter 3 Song
Psalm 150:1-6

1 – Praise ye the Lord, praise God in his sanctuary: praise him in the firmament of his power.

2 – Praise him for his mighty acts; praise him according to his excellent greatness.

3 – Praise him with the sound of the trumpet: praise him with the psaltery and harp.

4 – Praise him with the timbrel and dance; praise him with the stringed instruments and organs.

5 – Praise him upon the loud cymbals: praise him upon the high-sounding cymbals.

6 – Let everything that hath breath praise the Lord, praise ye the Lord.

OT

Proverbs 11:30 The fruit of the righteous is a tree of life, and he that winneth souls is wise.

Chapter 4
What is the Cornerstone?

OT

Deuteronomy 32:4 He is our rock, his work is perfect; for all his ways are judgment; a God of truth and without iniquity, just and right is he.

II Samuel 22:32 For who is God, save the Lord? And who is a rock, save our God?

Psalm 18:2 The Lord is my rock, and my fortress, and my deliverer, my God, my strength, in whom I will trust, my buckler, and the horn of my salvation, and my high tower.

78:35 And they remembered that God was their rock, and the high God their redeemer.

89:26 He shall cry out unto me, thou art my Father, my God, and the rock of my salvation.

Isaiah 17;10 Because thou has forgotten the God of thy salvation, and hast not been mindful of thy strength, rock, therefore shall thou plant pleasant plants, and shall set it with strange slips.

28:16 Therefore thus saith the Lord God, behold, I lay in Zion for a foundation, a stone, a tried stone, a precious cornerstone, a sure foundation; he that believeth shall not make haste.

Daniel 2:47 The King answered unto Daniel, and saith, of a truth it is, that your God is a God of gods, and a Lord of kings, and a revealer of secrets, seeing thou reveal secrets.

Zechariah 14:9 And the Lord shall be King over all the Earth, in that day shall there be one Lord, and his name one.

Malachi 1:11 For from the rising of the sun even unto the going down of the same my name shall be great among the Gentiles.

4:5 Behold I will send Elijah, the prophet before the coming of the great and dreadful day of the Lord.

Isaiah 9:6 For unto us a child is born, unto us a son is given; his name shall be called, The Mighty God, The Everlasting Father, The Prince of Peace.

NT

Matthew 1:22 Now all this was done, that it might be fulfilled which was spoken of the Lord by the prophecy, saying; Verse 23 Behold, a virgin shall be with child, and bring forth a son, and they shall call his name Emmanuel, which interpreted is, God with us.

16:18 And I say also unto thee, that thou art Peter, and upon this rock I will build (my church); and the gates of Hell shall not prevail against it.

Mark 12:29 And Jesus answered him, the first of all the commandments is, Hear O Israel; the Lord our God is one Lord.

16:16 He that believeth and is baptized shall be saved; but he that believeth not shall be damned; Verse 17 And these signs shall follow them that believe, in my name shall they cast out devils; they shall speak with new tongues.

Acts 2:4 And they were all filled with the Holy Ghost, and began to speak with other tongues, as the Spirit gave them utterance.

John 10:30 I and my Father are one.

Acts 20:28 Take heed therefore unto yourselves, and to all the flock, over which the Holy Ghost, hath made you overseers, to feed the church of God, which he hath purchased with his own blood.

Ephesians 2:20 And are built upon the foundation of the apostles and prophets, Jesus Christ himself being the chief cornerstone.

Philippians 2:6 Who, being in the form of God, thought it not robbery to be equal with God.

John 20:22 And when he had said this, he breathed on them, and said unto them, receive the Holy Ghost.

Hebrews 12:2 Looking unto Jesus the author and finisher of our faith.

Mark 12:29 And Jesus answered him, the first of all the commandments is, hear, O Israel; the Lord our God is one Lord.

I Timothy 3:16 And without controversy (great is the mystery of godliness, God was manifest in the flesh) justified in the Spirit, seen of angels, preached unto the Gentiles, believed on in the world, received up into glory.

Hebrews 5:9 And being made perfect, he became the author of eternal salvation unto all them that obey him.

Acts 4:12 Neither is there salvation in any other; for there is none other name whereby we must be saved.

4:12 This is the stone which was set at nought of you builders, which is become the head of the corner.

What A Mighty God We Serve
Song

What a mighty God we serve,
What a mighty God we serve,
Angels bow before Him,
Heaven and Earth adore him.
What a mighty God we serve,
What a mighty God we serve,
Angels bow before Him,
Heaven and Earth adore him.

OT

Daniel 12:4 But thou, O Daniel, shut up the words, and seal the book, even to the time of the end: many shall run to and fro, and knowledge shall be increased.

Malachi 1:11 For from the rising of the sun even unto the going down of the same my name shall be great among the Gentiles; and in every place incense shall be offered unto my name, and a pure offering: for my name shall be great among the heathen: saith the Lord of hosts.

NT

Matthew 1:21 And she shall bring forth a son, and thou shall call his name Jesus: for he shall save his people from their sins.

OT

Exodus 6:3 And I appeared unto Abraham, unto Isaac, and unto Jacob, by the name of God Almighty; but my name Jehovah was I not known to them.

NT

1:17 And when I saw him, I fell at his feet as dead. And he laid his right hand upon me, saying unto me, Fear not; I am the first and the last.

1:18 I am he that liveth and was dead; and behold, I am alive forever more, amen; and have the keys of Hell and death.

Matthew 11:25 Jesus said unto her, I am the resurrection, and the life.

Chapter 5
How Do you Know You're Saved?

NT

John 3:5 Jesus answered and said unto him, verily, verily, I say unto thee, except a man be born again, he cannot see the Kingdom of God.

12:32 And I, if I be lifted up from the Earth, will draw all men to me.

Acts 2:38 Then Peter said unto them, repent, and be baptized every one of you in the name of Jesus Christ, for the remission of sins, and ye shall receive the gift of the Holy Ghost; Verse 39 For the promise is unto you, and to your children, and to all that are afar off, even as many as the Lord our God shall call; Verse 41 Then they that gladly received his word were baptized; and the same day there were added unto them about 3,000 souls.

Acts 19:2-6 He said unto them, have ye received the Holy Ghost since ye believed? And they said unto him, we have not so much as heard whether there be and Holy Ghost; Verse

3 And he said unto them, Unto what then were ye baptized? And they said, Unto John's baptism; Verse 4 Then said Paul, John verily baptized with the baptism of repentance, saying unto the people, that they should believe on him which should come after him, that is Christ Jesus; Verse 5 When they heard this, they were baptized in the name of the Lord Jesus; Verse 6 And when Paul laid his hands upon them, the Holy Ghost came on them; and they spoke with tongues, and prophesying.

OT

Proverbs 3:5 Trust in the Lord with all thine heart; and lean not unto thine own understanding.

Isaiah 28:9 To whom shall he teach knowledge? And whom shall he make to understand (doctrine)? Them that are weaned from the milk and drawn from the breasts; Verse 10 For precept must be upon precept, precept upon precept, line upon line, here a little, and there a little; Verse 11 For with stammering lips and another (tongue) will he speak to his people.

Isaiah 55:6 Seek ye the Lord while he may be found, call ye upon him while he is near.

Psalm 124:8 Our help is in the (name) of the Lord, who made Heaven and Earth. Please, let us go to the sinner's prayer, I now accept Jesus Christ as my savior.

NT

Acts 8:13 Then Simon himself believed also, and when he was baptized, he continued with Phillip, and wondered, beholding the miracles and signs done; Verse 15 Who, when they were come down, prayed for them, that they might receive the Holy Ghost; Verse 16 (For as yet he was fallen upon none of them; only they were baptized in the name of the Lord Jesus).

Now we see here, he had faith, was baptized, yet he wasn't

saved.

John 3:5 Jesus answered, and said, Except a man be born of water and of the (Spirit), he cannot enter into the Kingdom of Heaven.

Acts 10:44 While Peter yet spoke these words, the Holy Ghost fell on them all, which heard the word; Verse 45 And they of the circumcision which believed were astonished, as many as came with Peter, because that on the Gentiles also was poured out the gift of the Holy Ghost; Verse 46 For they heard them speak with tongues and magnify God. Then Peter answered; Verse 47 Can any man forbid water, that these should not be baptized, which have received the Holy Ghost (as well as we); Verse 48 And he commanded them to be baptized in the name of the Lord.

Most preachers today believe in speaking in tongues, they don't teach others, but…

Acts 2:38 Then Peter said unto them, repent, and be baptized every one of you in the name of Jesus Christ for the (remission of sins) and ye shall receive the gift of the Holy Ghost; Verse 39 For the promise is unto you, and to your children, (and to all that afar off) even as many as the Lord our God shall call; Verse 41 Then they that (received) the word (gladly) were baptized, 3,000 souls were added.

Yes, today many churches preach Apostolic, Apostles Doctrine, Jesus said we all must be born of (water and Spirit).

John 3:3-8 Kingdom of God.

Matthew 4:17 From that time Jesus began to preach and to say, repent for the Kingdom of Heaven is at hand.

6:33 But seek ye first the Kingdom of God, and his righteousness; and all things shall be added to you.

7:21 Not everyone that saith unto me, Lord, shall enter into the Kingdom of Heaven; but he that doeth the will of my Father which is in Heaven; Verse 22 Many will say to me in that day, Lord, Lord, have we not prophesied in thy name? And in thy name have cast out devils? And in thy name done many wonderful works?

NT

Matthew 7:23 And then I will (say) profess unto them, I never knew you; depart from me, ye that work iniquity.

Luke 11:13 If ye then, being evil, know how to give good gifts unto your children; how much more shall your Father give the Holy Ghost to them that ask him? (Spirit)

John 3:5 Jesus answered, verily, verily, I say unto thee, except a man be born of (water) and of the (Spirit), he cannot enter into the Kingdom of God.

John 5:39 Search the scriptures: for in them ye think ye have eternal life: and they are they which testify of me; Verse 40 And ye will not come to me, that you might have life.

Hebrews 5:9 And being perfect, he became the author of eternal salvation unto them that obey him.

Matthew 16:18 And I say unto thee, thou art Peter, and upon this rock I will build my church; and the gates of Hell shall not prevail against it; Verse 19 And I will give you the keys of the Kingdom of Heaven; and whatsoever thou shalt bind on Earth shall be bound in Heaven; and whatsoever (who) thou lose on Earth loosed in Heaven.

John 21:15-17 Feed my sheep.

Acts 2:4 And they were all filled with the Holy Ghost (Spirit) and began to speak with other tongues, as the (Spirit) gave them utterance; Verse 14-41 But Peter, standing up with the eleven, lifted up his voice. Peter's keys to Heaven was shaken. He obeyed Jesus's command to feed sheep; Verse 37 Now when they heard this, they were pricked in their heart, and said unto Peter and to the rest of the apostles, men and brethren, what shall we do?; Verse 38 Then Peter said unto them, (repent) and be (baptized) every one of you in the name of (Jesus Christ) for the (remission of sins) and ye shall receive the gift of the Holy Ghost; Verse 39 For the promise is unto (you, and to your children, and to all that are afar off), even as many as our Lord our God shall call.

John 3:5 (Water and Spirit)

Some people say it was just for those 12 apostles, Bible says for all. Many churches today still preach Saint Peter's words or keys to Kingdom. Most leaders in today's far off times speak in tongues, some still do baptize in Jesus's lovely name, they can cast out demons and devils in Jesus's lovely name, Jesus told us we can do this or that in His name.

John 3:5 Jesus said, verily, verily, I say unto you, except a man be born of water and of the Spirit, he cannot enter into the Kingdom of God.

Luke 23:42 And he said unto Jesus, Lord, remember me when thou comest into thy Kingdom.

Mark 2:10 But that ye may know that the (Son of Man) hath power on Earth to forgive sins.

The Bible was written by Moses and the prophets, apostles, Jesus Christ himself, the Chief Cornerstone.

Ephesians 2:20 Those all died, apostles feeding the faith.

Act 2:38-42 For all, even afar off, the old Devil and his demons doesn't care if we cast out them, they just don't want (us all) to be born of (water and Spirit).

John 3:5

II Corinthians 10:13-14 For such are false apostles, deceitful workers, transforming themselves into the apostles of Christ;

Verse 14 And no marvel; for Satan himself is transformed expressly, that in latter times (far off) some shall depart from the faith, giving heed to seducing spirits, and doctrines of devils.

Where is Jesus's name in baptism today, Devil tries to kill, steal and destroy, it's time to put (Jesus's name) back in baptism. We do everything else in Jesus's lovely salvation-saving name. Raise your hand, believe and you're saved, faith without work is dead.

Acts 2:38 Doesn't say that, Apostle Peter feed those sheep, to us all even all afar off, as many as our Lord God shall call.

Matthew 24:11 And many false prophets shall rise, and shall deceive many.

How many churches today baptize in Jesus's lovely name? Most churches don't believe when you receive the (Holy Ghost) Spirit that you will speak in tongues. First church believed 3,000 souls added. Apostle Peter, plus 120 others received Holy Ghost filling, Apostle Paul wrote and tried to warn all that false apostles would try to destroy church. Where is Jesus's name, Apostolic churches today preach the…

Acts 2:38-42 Where are you and family and friends spend eternal life, Heaven? He is waiting on all afar off, to get born of water and Spirit.

John 3:5

Proverbs 3:5 Trust in the Lord with all thine heart; and (lean not unto thine own understanding).

Philippians 2:12 Work out your own salvation with fear and trembling.

Acts 2:38-42

John 3:5

Revelation 20:6,7 Jesus name saves.

Luke 22:29-32

OT

Psalm 23:1 the Lord is my shepherd, I shall not want.

2 He maketh me to lie down in green pastures; he leadeth me beside the still waters.

3 He restores my soul: he leadeth me in the paths of righteousness for His name's sake.

4 Yea, though I walk through the valley of the shadow of death, I will fear no evil: for thou art with me; thy rod and thy staff they comfort me.

5 Thou preparest a table before me in the presence of mine enemies: thou anointest my head with oil, my cup runneth over.

6 Surely goodness and mercy shall follow me all the days of my life and I will dwell in the house of the Lord forever.

NT

I Thessalonians 4:13 But I would not have you to be ignorant, brethren, concerning them which are asleep, that you sorrow not, even as others which have no hope.

14 For if we believe that Jesus died and arose again, even so them also which sleep in Jesus will God bring with him.

15 For this we say unto you by the word of the Lord, that we which are alive and remain unto the coming of the Lord shall not prevent them which are asleep.

16 For the Lord himself shall descend from Heaven with a shout, with the voice of the archangel, and with the trump of God: and the dead in Christ shall rise first.

17 Then we which are alive and remain shall be caught up together with them in the clouds, to meet the Lord in the air: and so shall we ever be with the Lord.

18 Wherefore comfort one another with these words.

Chapter 6 - Where Are the Dead?

OT

Genesis 2:7 And the Lord God formed man of the dust of the ground, and breathed into his nostrils the breath of life; and man became a living soul; Verse 17 But of the tree of the knowledge of good and evil, thou shall not eat of it: for in the day that thou eatest there of thou shalt surely die.

3:6 And when the woman saw that the tree was good for food, and that it was pleasant to the eyes, and a tree to be desired to make one wise, she took of the fruit thereof, and did eat, and gave also unto her husband with her, and he did eat; Verse 19 In the sweat of thy face shalt thou eat bread, till thou return unto the ground; for out of it wast thou taken; for dust thou art, and unto dust shall thou return.

5:5 And all the days that Adam lived were nine hundred and thirty years: and he died.

5:23,24 And all the days of Enoch were 365 years; Verse 24 And Enoch walked with God; and he was not; for God took him.

25:8 Then Abraham gave up the ghost, and died, is a good old age, and old man, and full of years; and was gathered to his people.

50:25,26 And Joseph took an oath of the children of Israel, saying, God will surely visit you, and ye shall carry up my bones from hence; Verse 26 So Joseph died, being a hundred and ten years old; and them embalmed him, and he was put in a coffin in Egypt.

Exodus 6:2 And God spoke unto Moses, and said unto him, I am the Lord.

13:18,19 But God led the people about, through the way of the wilderness of the Red Sea: and the children of Israel went up harnessed out of Egypt; Verse 19 And Moses took the bones of Joseph with him; for he had straitly sworn the children of Israel, saying, God will surely visit you, and ye shall carry up my bones away from hence, with you.

Deuteronomy 34:5 And Moses the servant of the Lord died there in the land of Moab, according to the word of the Lord.

I Samuel 28:3 Now Samuel was dead, and all Israel had lamented him, and buried him in Ramah, in his own city. And Saul had put away those that had familiar spirits, and the wizards, out of the land; Verse 13-15 And the King said unto her, be not afraid: for what sawest thou? And the (witch) woman said unto Saul, I saw gods ascending out of the Earth; Verse 14 And he said unto her, what form is he of? And she said, an old man cometh up; and he is covered with a mantle; and Saul perceived that it was Samuel, and he stooped his face to the ground, and bowed himself; Verse 15 And Samuel said to Saul, why hast thou disquieted me, and to bring me up? And Saul answered, I am distressed; for the Philistines make war against me, and God is departed from me, and answereth me no more, neither by prophets, nor by dreams, therefore I have called thee, that thou mayest make known what I shall do.

II Kings 2:9-11 Verse 9 And it came to pass, when they were gone over, that Elijah said unto Elisha, ask what I shall do for thee, before I be taken away from thee, and Elisha said, I pray thee, let a double portion of thy Spirit be upon me; Verse 10 And he said, thou hast asked a hard thing, nevertheless, if thou see me when I am taken from thee, it shall be so unto thee; but if not, it shall not be; Verse 11 And it came to pass, as they still went on, and talked, and behold, there appeared a chariot of fire, and horses of fire, and parted them both asunder, and Elijah went up by a whirlwind into Heaven.

Ecclesiastes 3:2 A time to be born, and a time to die; a time to plant, and a time to puck up that which is planted.

8:8 There is no man that hath power over the Spirit to retain the Spirit; neither hath the power in the day of death; and there is no discharge in that war, neither shall wickedness deliver those that are given to it.

9:5 For the living know that they shall die; but the dead know not anything, neither have they anymore a reward for the memory of them is forgotten.

12:7 Then shall the dust return to the Earth as it was; and the Spirit shall return unto God who gave it.

Isaiah 55:6 Seek ye the Lord while he may be found, call ye upon him while he's near.

46:9,10 Remember the former things of old: for I am God, and there is none else; I am God, and there is none like me; Verse 10 Declaring the end from the beginning, and from ancient times the things that are not yet done, saying, my counsel shall stand, and I will do all my pleasures.

7:14 Therefore the Lord himself shall give you a sign; behold a virgin shall conceive, and bear a son, and shall call his name Immanuel.

9:6 For unto us a child is born, unto us a son is given, and the government shall be upon his shoulder; and his name shall be called Wonderful, Counsellor, the Mighty God, the Everlasting Father, the Prince of Peace.

Malachi 4:5 I will send you Elijah the prophet before the coming of the great and dreadful day of the Lord.

Genesis 5: This is the book of generations of Adam. In the day that God created man, in the likeness of God made he him.

5:5 And all the days that Adam lived were nine hundred and thirty years: and he died.

6:1 And it came to pass, when men began to multiply on the face of the Earth, and daughters were born unto them.

6:5 And God saw that the wickedness of man was great in the Earth and that every imagination of the thoughts of the heart was evil continually.

6:7 And the Lord said, I will destroy man whom I have created from the face of the Earth; both man and beast, and the creeping thing, and the fowls of the air, for it repenteth me that I have made them.

6:8 But Noah found grace in the eyes of the Lord.

6:18 But with thee, I will establish my covenant, and thou shalt come into the ark, thou, and thy sons, and thy wife, and thy son's wives with thee.

9:28 And Noah lived after the flood 350 years; Verse 29 And all the days of Noah were 950 years and he died.

NT

Matthew 1:23 Behold, a virgin shall be with child, and shall bring forth a son, and they shall call his name Emmanuel, which being interpreted is God with us; Verse 25 Then Joseph being raised from sleep did as the angel of the Lord had bidden him, and took unto him his wife; Verse 25 And knew her not till she had brought forth her firstborn son; and called his name Jesus.

3:1 In those days came John the Baptist, preaching in the wilderness of Judaea; Verse 13 then cometh Jesus from Galilee to Jordan unto John, to be baptized of thee, and cometh thou unto me?; Verse 15 And Jesus answering said unto him, suffer it to be now: for thus it becometh us to fulfill all righteousness. Then he suffered him; Verse 16 And Jesus, when he was baptized, went up straightway out of the water; and lo, the heavens were opened unto him, and he saw the Spirit of God descending like a dove, and lighting upon him; Verse 17 And a voice from Heaven, saying, this is my beloved Son, in whom I am well pleased.

4:1 Then was Jesus led up of the Spirit into the wilderness to be tempted of the Devil; Verse 2 And when he fasted 40 days and 40 nights.

4:17 From that time Jesus began to preach, and to say, repent; for the Kingdom of Heaven is at hand.

9:23 And when Jesus came into the ruler's house, and saw the minstrels and the people making a noise; Verse 24 He said unto them, Give place; for the maid is not dead, but sleepeth, and they laughed him to scorn; Verse 25 But when the people were put forth, he went in, and took her by the hand, and the maid arose.

17:1 And after 6 days Jesus taketh Peter, James, and John his brother, and bringeth them up to a high mountain apart, and was transfigured before them, and his face did shine as the sun, and his raiment was white as the light; Verse 3 And behold, there appeared unto them Moses and Elias talking with him.

John 11:11 These things said he: and after that be saith unto them, our friend Lazarus sleepeth; but I go, that I may awaken him out of sleep.

14 Then said Jesus unto them plainly, Lazarus is dead; Verse 23 Jesus said unto her, thy brother shall rise again; Verse 24 Martha said unto him, I know that he shall rise again in the resurrection, at the last day; Verse 25 Jesus said unto her, I am the resurrection, and the life: he that believeth in me shall never die, though he was dead, yet shall he live; Verse 43 And when he thus had spoken, he cried with a loud voice, Lazarus come forth; Verse 44 And he that was dead came forth, bound hand and foot, with grave clothes, and his face was bound about with a napkin, Jesus said unto them, loose him, and let him go.

Acts 20:9 And there sat in a window a certain young man named Eutychus, being fallen into a deep sleep, and as Paul was long preaching, he sunk down with sleep, and fell down from the third loft, and was taken up dead; Verse 10 And Paul went down, and fell on him, and embracing him said, trouble not yourselves, for his life is in him.

Romans 8:11 But if the Spirit of him that raised up Jesus from the dead dwell in you, he that raised up Christ from the dead shall also quicken your mortal bodies by his Spirit that dwelleth in you.

Corinthians 15:20 but now is Christ risen from the dead, and become the first fruits of them that slept; Verse 51 Behold, I show you a mystery. We shall not all sleep, but we shall be changed.

52 In a moment, in the twinkling of an eye, at the last trump; for the trumpet shall sound, and the dead shall be raised incorruptible, and we shall be changed.

I Thessalonians 4:13 But I would not have you to be

ignorant, brethren, concerning them which are a(sleep), that ye sorrow not, even as others which have no hope; Verse 14 For if we believe that Jesus died and arose again, even so them also which sleep in Jesus will God bring with him; Verse 15 For this we say by the word of the Lord, that we which are alive and unto the coming of the Lord shall not prevent them which are asleep; Verse 16 For the Lord Himself shall descend from Heaven with a shout, with the voice of the archangel, and with the trump of God; and the dead in Christ shall rise first; Verse 17 Then we which are alive and remain shall be caught up together with them in the clouds, to meet the Lord in the air: and so shall we ever be with him.

II Peter 3:10 But the day of the Lord will come as a thief in the night; in which the heavens shall pass away with a great noise, and the elements shall melt with fervent heat, the Earth also and the works that are therein shall be burned up; Verse 11 Seeing then that all these things shall be dissolved, what manner of persons ought ye to be in all (holy conversation and Godliness); Verse 12 Looking for the hasting unto the coming of the day of God, wherein the heavens being on fire shall be dissolved, and the elements shall melt with fervent heat?; Verse 13 Nevertheless we, according to his promise, look for the new heavens and a new Earth, wherein dwelleth righteousness.

Revelation 21:1 And I saw a new Heaven and a new Earth: for the first Heaven and the first Earth were passed away; and there was no more sea.

1:2 And I John saw the holy city, new Jerusalem, coming down from God out of Heaven, prepared as a bride adorned for his husband.

OT

As we read, we see a few went to Heaven, II Kings 2:11

Elijah.

Genesis 5:24 Enoch, walked with God, for God took him.

Exodus 13:19 Moses took Joseph's bones out of Egypt.

I Samuel 28:15 Saul woke Samuel up from his (sleep, death).

Job 38:17 Have the gates of death been opened unto thee? Or has thou seen the doors of the (shadow of death)?

NT

Luke 23:44 Today shalt thou be with me in paradise.

John 11:25 Jesus said unto her, I am the resurrection, and the life;

11:43 Lazarus come forth; Verse 44 And he that was dead came forth.

Matthew 27:52,53 And the graves were opened; and many of bodies of the saints which slept arose and came out of the graves after his resurrection, and went into the Holy City, and appeared unto many.

John 8:51 Verily, Verily, I say unto you, if a man keep my saying, he shall never see death (sleep).

Questions — True or False

1.(A) Is Jesus Lord? True or False
(B) Did Jesus die for sins? True or False
2.(A) Did Apostle Peter have keys to the Kingdom of Heaven? True or False
(B) Did Apostle Peter say Acts 2:38,39 was for all? True or False
3.(A) Is faith enough to save us? True or False
(B) Did faith save Simon when he believed in Acts 8:13-19? True or False
4.(A) Does water baptism now save us (Peter 3:21)? True or False
(B) Did Jesus say in Mark 16:16 He that believed and is baptized shall be saved; and he that believeth not shall be damned? True or False
5.(A) In John 3:5 did Jesus say, Except a man be born of water and Spirit, he cannot enter into Heaven? True or False
6.(A) Do you need to be baptized in Jesus's name after you repent (Acts 2:38,39)? True or False

(B) Was that just for them? True or False - Or for all? True or False

7.(A) Was the Holy Ghost promised to all? True or False

(B) Do you speak in tongues when you receive the gift of the Holy Ghost, as in Acts 2:4,41, 10:43-48, 11:14-21, 19:1-6? True or False

8.(A) If I was already baptized, should I get baptized in Jesus's name, as in Acts 19:1-5,6? True or False

(B) Did a man in II Kings 5:10 be told to get in water 7 times to become clean? Verse 14, Then he dipped 7 times. True or False

9.(A) In Daniel 12:4, even to the time of the end, soon? True or False

(B) Is time about finished? Matthew 24:14 And this gospel of the Kingdom shall be preached in all the world for a witness unto all nations; and then shall the end come. True or False

Prayer for Pardon

OT

Psalm 51:1-17 Have mercy upon me, O God, according to thy loving kindness: according unto the multitude of thy tender mercies blot out my transgressions. 2 Wash me thoroughly from mine iniquity, and cleanse me from my sin. 3 For I acknowledge my transgressions: and my sin is ever before me. 4 Against thee, thee only, have I sinned, and done this evil in thy sight: that thou mightest be justified when thou speakest; and be clear hen thou judgest. 5 Behold, I was shapen in iniquity; and in sin did my mother conceive me. 6 Behold, thou desirest truth in the inward parts: and in the hidden part thou make me to know wisdom. 7 Purge me with hyssop and I shall be clean: wash me, and I shall be whiter than snow. 8 Make me to hear joy and gladness; that the bones which thou hast broken may rejoice. 9 Hide my face from my sins and blot out all mine iniquities. 10 Create in me a clean heart, O God, and renew a (right Spirit) within me. 11 Cast me not away from thy presence; and take not thy Holy Spirit from me. 12

Restore unto me the joy of thy salvation; and uphold me with thy free Spirit. 13 Then (will I) teach transgressors thy ways, and sinners shall be converted unto thee. 14 Deliver me from blood-guiltness, O God, thou God, of my salvation: and my tongue shall sing aloud of thy righteousness. 15 O Lord, open thou my lips; and my mouth shall shew forth thy praise. 16 For thou desirest not sacrifice; else would I give it: thou delightest not in burnt offering. 17 The sacrifices of God are a broken Spirit; a broken and a contrite heart, O God, thou will not despise.

Proverbs 3:5 Trust in the Lord with all thine heart; and lean not unto thine own understanding. 11:30 The fruit of the righteous is a tree of life; and he that winneth souls is wise.

NT

Luke 15:10 Likewise, I say unto you, there is joy in the presence of the angels of God over one sinner that repenteth.

Acts 2:38 Then Peter said unto them, repent, and be baptized every one of you in the name of Jesus Christ for the remission of sins, and ye shall receive the gift of the Holy Ghost.

Chapter 7 - True Christmas Story

As I grew up, I looked forward to Christmas holidays. The nice pine trees, oh, the wonderful fresh smell, the silver and gold trims, the blinking lights, the glass bulbs, that star of light on the tiptop.

We were taught Jesus was born on that merry day of the year. In time, everyone looked forward to that eve. We knew Santa Claus would bring us all those precious gifts, oh, the fun and great times we had as a family. The best of all year meal, the family came together, as eve and Xmas day.

No one truly understood that it was a sinful time, brought through time, handed down from Old Testament Jeremiah 10:1: Hear ye the word which the Lord speaketh unto you, O house of Israel. 2 Thou saith the Lord, learn not the way of the heathen, and be not dismayed at the signs of Heaven; for the heathen are dismayed at them. 3 For the customs of the people are vain; for one cutteth a tree out of the forest, the work of the hands of the workman, with the axe. 4 They deck it with silver and gold; they fasten it with nails and hammers, that it will not move.

As I sadly read these words, I quit that day of fun. We tell our kids about Santa and sled and reindeers, the North Pole home. Giving gifts should be all the year long, presents are truly wonderful. Jesus gave us the special gift, once and for all, the forgiveness of sins. We want Jesus to forgive us all for our sins and failures in this life. But who truly forgives a man or woman for their failures in life? Yes, we all say, "But you don't know what they did (past tense) in life." Jesus told his disciples that they should forgive 7x70 times. It wasn't just for those days, he said that phrase for all mankind, hard thing to do, but true. How many chances should Jesus give us? I hoped and prayed my 7 times was 70 times. I know that cross took all my 7x70 sins away. Grace and mercy we desire, but do we truly give it to others? Why put off today when tomorrow isn't promised?

As we go into this year, let us all start praising and thanking Jesus for the cross.

NT

Matthew 6-19.9 After this manner therefore pray ye: our Father which is in Heaven, hallowed be thou name. 10 Thy Kingdom come, thy will be done on Earth as it is in Heaven. 11 Give us this day our daily bread. 12 And forgive us our debts, as we forgive our debtors.

Who wants God's forgiveness?

CHAPTER 8
WHO WILL FEED MY SHEEP?

As I watch the television and listen to the Big-Name Preachers, they often speak about themself receiving the Holy Ghost, by speaking in tongues, born of the Spirit. Apostles who loved Jesus spoke up, they told three thousand souls how to receive the Holy Ghost by speaking in tongues. Sadly, today these preachers aren't like those Apostles Peter, Paul, and so many other true SAINTS who gave up their lives to feed Jesus's hungry sheep.

Jesus said in Matthew 5:14 Ye are the light of the world. A city that is set on a hill cannot be hidden. Verse 15 Neither do men light a candle and put it under a bushel, but on a candlestick, and it giveth light unto (all) that are in the house. 16 Let your light so shine before men, that they may see your good works, and glorify your Father, which is in Heaven.

Acts 2:38-42 Then Peter said unto them, repent, and be baptized every one of you in the name of Jesus Christ (for the remission of your sins) and ye shall receive the gift of the

Holy Ghost. Verse 39 For the promise is unto you, and to your children, and to (all) that are afar off, even as many as the Lord our God shall call. Verse 41 Then they that gladly received his word were baptized, and the same day there were about 3,000 souls added.

Acts 9:1-21 Saul to Apostle Paul, look how God used that man. Apostle Paul fed those hungry sheep.

Acts 19:1-6 20:28 Take heed therefore unto yourselves, and to all the flock, over which the Holy Ghost hath made you overseers, to feed the church of God, which he hath purchased with his own blood.

Those apostles loved Jesus, do you love Jesus? You preachers that have the (Spirit) Holy Ghost, you're born of Spirit. Like John 3:5 halfway to Heaven, but you still need to be baptized in Jesus's lovely name. Saint Peter said for all, not just those pride.

Acts 26:23-28 King Agrippa believed, but he would not obey, so his own pride took him, his family, and friends to Hell. Jesus is looking for apostles today to feed his sheep.

Let us state this clearly by the scriptures, as Jesus states.

NT

John 15:16 Ye have not chosen me, but I have chosen you, and ordained you, that you should go and bring forth fruit, and that your fruit should remain; that whatsoever ye shall ask of the Father in my name, he may give it to you.

God chooses whosoever He will, Moses to the last prophet. The Bible was written by those holy prophets, apostles, they all fell short of the glory. Moses was 40 years old when God called him to start. Every man or woman God calls isn't of the perfect image of Jesus until Jesus shapes and molds that person, creates a right mind and heart, then fills him with the

Holy Ghost, fit for God's purpose for His Kingdom. God looks at his future heart and mind, He (only) knows our future.

Jesus picked Judas knowing he would betray him for 30 pieces of silver. Look at Apostle Peter, lied 3 times, I never knew him, oh, how sad. Apostle Paul, destroying those blessed apostles to death, terrible man.

Once Jesus fills you with the Holy Ghost, you're fit for His Kingdom. God is calling His far-off preachers today, who shall lead these sheep. They are ready, they just need a pull out of the darkness into the light. Moses didn't think he was fit, but God knew Moses would finish, just like He knows each one of ours, just like the US Marines calling, God is looking for a few good men. Who will step froward in these far-off days, proud to do work for the Kingdom to come? Don't put off today, or tomorrow isn't promised. If you're waiting to be perfect, then God will not use you. He is perfect. He alone is perfect. All fall short of the glory, from Adam and Eve to the last man.

Everyone born into this world was born a sinner because of Adam's fault. Thank God we can be created into Christ's image, fit for His Kingdom. Don't think you are better than those prophets or apostles or Moses, humble yourself, lean not unto your own understanding. Today you can search for Truth, when every church started in history in less than an hour get ready before the 7-year terrible tribulation. If you love your family and friends and church, lead them to God's Kingdom, get them out of the darkness into Jesus's light, quicken.

Chapter 9 - The Serpent or Sin

OT

Genesis 3:1-15 Now the serpent was more subtle than any beast of the field which the Lord God had made. And he said unto the woman, yea, hath God said, yea shall not eat of every tree of the garden? 2 And the woman said unto serpent, we may eat of the fruit of the trees of the garden. 3 But of the fruit of the tree which is in the midst of the garden, God hath said, ye shall not eat of it, neither shall ye touch it, lest ye die. 4 And the serpent said unto the woman, ye shall not surely die. 5 For God doth know that in the day ye eat thereof, then your eyes shall be opened, and ye shall be as gods, knowing good and evil. 6 And when the woman saw that the tree was good for food, and that it was pleasant to the eyes, and a tree to be desired to make one wise, she took of the fruit thereof, and did eat, and gave also unto her husband with her, and he did eat. 7 And the eyes of them both were opened, and they knew that they were naked; and they sewed fig leaves together, and made themselves aprons. 8 And they heard the voice of the

Lord, god walking in the garden in the cool of the day: and Adam and his wife hid themselves from the presence of the Lord God amongst the trees of the garden. 9 And the Lord God called unto Adam, and said unto him, where art thou? 10 And he said, I heard thy voice in the garden, and I was afraid because I was naked; and I hid myself. 11 And he said, who told thee that thou was naked? Hast thou eaten of the tree whereof I commanded thee that you shouldest not eat? 12 And the man said, the woman whom thou gavest to be with me, she gave me of the tree, and I did eat. 14 And the Lord God said unto the (serpent), because thou hast done this, thou art cursed above all cattle, and above every beast of the field; upon thy belly shall thou go, and dust shalt thou eat all the days of thy life. 15 And I will put enmity between thee and the woman, and between thy seed and her seed; it shall bruise thy head, and thou shalt bruise his heal.

Numbers 21:5 And the people spoke against God and Moses. Wherefore have ye brought us out of Egypt to die in the wilderness? For there is no bread, neither is there any water; and our soul loatheth this light bread. 6 And the Lord sent (fiery serpents) among the people, and they bit the people; and much people of Israel died. 7 Therefore, the people came to Moses and said, we have sinned, for we have spoken against the Lord and against thee; pray unto the Lord that he take away the (serpents) from us. And Moses prayed for the people. 8 And the Lord said unto Moses, make thee a (fiery serpent) and set it upon a pole; and it shall come to pass that everyone that is bitten, when he looketh upon it, shall live. 9 And Moses made a (serpent of brass) and put it upon a pole, and it came to pass that if a (serpent) bit any man, when he beheld the (serpent of brass) he lived.

Deuteronomy 20:22 And if a man have committed sin worthy of death, and he be put to death, and thou hang him on a tree.

Isaiah 7: Therefore, the Lord Himself shall give you a sign: behold a virgin shall conceive and bear a son, and shall call his name Immanuel.

Malachi 4:5 Behold, I will send you Elijah the prophet before the coming of the great and dreadful day of the Lord.

NT

Matthew 1:21 And she shall bring forth a son, and thou shalt call his name Jesus: for he shall save his people from their sins. 1:22 Now all this was done that it might be fulfilled which was spoken of the Lord by the prophet saying, 23 Behold, a virgin shall be with child and shall bring forth a son, and they shall call his name Emmanuel, which being interpreted is God with us. 24 Then Joseph being raised from sleep did as the angel of the Lord had bidden him and took unto him his wife. 25 And knew her not till she had brought forth her firstborn son: and he called his name Jesus.

John 19: When Jesus had received the vinegar, he said, it is finished; and he bowed his head and gave up the ghost. 20:11 But Mary stood without the sepulchre weeping and as she wept, she stooped down and looked into the sepulchre. 12 And seeth two angels in white sitting, the one at the head and the other at the feet, where the body of Jesus had lain. 15 Jesus said unto her, woman, why weepest thou?

Romans 5:14 Nevertheless death reigned from Adam to Moses, even over them that had not sinned after the similitude of Adam's transgression, who is the figure of him that was to come.

Romans 5:19 For as by one man's disobedience many were

made sinners, so by the obedience of one man shall be made righteous.

I Corinthians 1:18 For the preaching of the cross is to them that perish, foolishness; but unto us which are saved it is the power of God. 10:8 Neither let us commit fornication, as some of them committed, and fell in one day three and twenty thousand. 9 Neither let us tempt Christ, as some of them also tempted, and were destroyed by serpents.

I Corinthians 10:2 And were all baptized into Moses in the cloud and in the sea (water).

I Peter 3:20 Which sometimes were disobedient, when once the longsuffering of God waited in the days of Noah, while the ark was a preparing, wherein few, that is eight souls, were saved by water. 3:21 The like figure where unto even baptism doth also now save us (not the putting away of filth of the flesh, but the answer of a good conscience toward God) by the resurrection of Jesus Christ.

I Corinthians 15:21 For since by man came death, by man came also the resurrection of the dead. 15:22 For as in Adam all die, even so in Christ shall all be made alive. 15:45 And so it is written, the first man Adam was made a living soul; the last Adam was made a quickening Spirit. 15:46 Howbeit that was not first which is spiritual, but that which is natural; and afterward that which is spiritual. 15:47 The first man is of the Earth, earthy; the second man is the Lord from Heaven. 15:48 As in the earthy, such are they also that are earthy; and as in the heavenly, such are they also that are heavenly. 15:49 And as we have borne the image of the earthy, we shall also bear the image of the heavenly. 15:50 Now this I say, brethren, that flesh and blood cannot inherit the Kingdom of God; neither doth corruption inherit incorruption. 15:51 Behold, I show you a mystery; we shall not all sleep, but we shall all be changed. 15:52 In a moment, in the twinkling of an eye, at the last trump: for the trumpet shall sound, and the dead shall be raised incorruptible, and we shall be changed. 15:53 For this corruptible must put on incorruption, and this mortal must put on immortality.

I Corinthians 1:19 For it is written, I will destroy the wisdom of the wise, and will bring to nothing the understanding of the prudent.

Who wants to stay in the darkness? Who wants to come to the light? Turn your lights off tonight, walk around, see how many times you fall. That old Devil and demons wants us all in the darkness. He doesn't want us to find the light. He loves it when you or I stumble or keep falling, but Jesus wants us all to come out of darkness into light and truth. Blind leads the blind, light leads us all into Jesus's true light (words of truth).

I am the way, the truth, and the light of this world, amen. God isn't trying to take away nothing. He is trying to add more Holy Ghost filling to us all, just like we did to those apostles and first Jesus built churches he added then and now to all who obey. Apostle Paul wrote most of the New Testament once he was awakened from the darkness into Jesus's bright light. Oh, look how he finished the race.

There are many apostolic churches today that preach Saint Peter's (keys). Jesus wants us all in the cloud on that trumpet sound for saints. God isn't asking no one to change churches, but to preach apostle doctrine. So many followers each one of you preachers have this far off time. First church 3,000 souls were added back then, millions can be saved in this far off day times. I know God chose each one of you all, I've heard you say so on live T.V. broadcasting. Share that testimony with your churches, baptize them into Jesus's loving name, help them receive the same Holy Ghost filling, quickening from darkness to light, death to life.

Who loves Jesus? Who hates darkness? Who loves the light (word)? Jesus says come while there is light, the darkness isn't good. Call each preacher you know, work together like those apostles did. Spread the True Gospel to those hungry lost sheep, souls. Time to move is now, the old world shall soon end with a bang, blast. As of now, the world has enough power, 10 times, to blow this Earth up. Do you want to head you and family and churches into those gates? I know God wants us all to come marching in with those saints.

Amen and amen.

Chapter 10 - The Bible

Basic instructions before leaving Earth.
OT
Ecclesiastes 3:2 A time to be born, and a time to die; a time to plant, and a time to pluck up that which is planted; 9:5 For the living know that they shall die; 12:6 Or ever the silver cord be loosed, or the golden bowl be broken, or the pitcher be broken at the fountain, or the wheel broken at the cistern. 12:7 Then shall the dust return to the Earth as it was; and the Spirit return unto God who gave it.

Daniel 2:28 But there is a God in Heaven that revealeth secrets, and maketh known to the King Nebuchadnezzar what shall be in the latter day. Thy dream and the visions of thy head upon thy bed are these. 29-45 (Latter days.)

Joel 2:28,29 I will pour out my Spirit.
NT
Philippians 2:12 Wherefore, my beloved, work out your own salvation with fear and trembling.

Hebrews 9:27 And as it is appointed unto men once to die,

but after this the judgment.

John 3:5 Jesus answered, verily, verily, I say unto thee, except a man be born of (water) and of the (Spirit) he cannot enter into the Kingdom of God. 3:6 That which is born of the flesh is flesh; and that which is born of the (Spirit) is Spirit.

Acts 2:38 Then Peter said unto them, repent, and be baptized in the name of (Jesus Christ) for the remission of sins, and ye shall receive the gift of the Holy Ghost.

Acts 4:12 Neither is there salvation in any other (name) for there is none other name under Heaven given among men (whereby we must be saved).

Acts 8:14 Now when the apostles which were at Jerusalem heard that Samaria had received the word of God, they sent unto them (Peter and John) 8:15 Who when they were come down, prayed for them that they might receive the Holy Ghost. 16 (For as yet he was fallen upon none of them; only they were baptized in the name of the Lord Jesus.) 17 Then laid they their hands on them, and they received the Holy Ghost.

Acts 19:5,6 When they heard this, they were baptized in the (name of Jesus Christ). 6 And when Paul laid his hands upon them, the Holy Ghost came on them; (Spirit) and they spoke with tongues and prophesied. 7 And all the men were about seven.

Matthew 3:1 In those days came John the Baptist, preaching in this wilderness of Judaea. 3:2 And saying, repent ye: for the Kingdom of Heaven is at hand. 3:11 I indeed baptize you with water unto repentance: but he that cometh after me is mightier than I, whose shoes I am not worthy bear; he shall baptize you with the Holy Ghost, and with fire.

John 20:22 And when he said this, he breathed on them and said unto them, receive ye the Holy Ghost. 23 Whosoever sins ye remit, they are remitted unto them; and whosoever sins ye retain, they are retained.

Acts 1:15 And Peter stood up in the midst of the disciples and said, (the number about 120).

Acts 2:4 And they were all filled with the Holy Ghost and began to speak with other tongues as the Spirit gave them utterance.

Acts 2:37 What shall we do?

Acts 2:38 Then Peter said unto them, repent, and be baptized every one of you in the (name of Jesus Christ) (for the remission of sins) and ye shall receive the gift of the Holy Ghost. 39 For the promise is unto you, and to your children, and (to all that are afar off) even as many as the Lord oru God shall call.

The Bible clearly says in the Old Testament Isaiah 28:9-13 Whom shall he teach knowledge, and whom shall he make to understand (doctrine)? Them that are weaned from the milk and drawn from the breasts. 10 For precept must be upon precept, precept upon precept; line upon line, line upon line, here a little, and there a little. 11 For with stammering lips and another tongue will he speak to his people. 12 To whom he said, this is the rest where with ye may cause the weary to rest; and this is the refreshing; yet they would not hear. 13 But the word of the Lord was unto them precept upon precept, line upon line, here a little, and there a little, that they might be backward and taken.

NT

John 4:24 God is a Spirit; and they that worship him must worship him in (Spirit and truth).

John 6:7 Then Simon Peter answered him, Lord, to whom shall we go? Thou hast the words of eternal life. We can choose life or death, just like...

Acts 2:37-42 41 They that gladly received his word were baptized; and the same day 3,000 souls were added.

Acts 26:26-28 Then Agrippa said unto Paul, almost thou persuadest me. If Apostle Peter, Apostle Paul rebaptized them (all) into Jesus's lovely name, laid hands on them till they (all) spoke in tongues, you, your family, friends, and church can choose your eternal life.

Oh, how time really flies by us all, about 2,000 years since the first Christian Holy Rollers started; time is truly winding down. Soon it will be no more, just this wonderful eternal, eternal life. No more pain, no more sorrow, no more death, just love, peace, and joy. Our families can walk with Jesus, sing new songs, talk to Adam and Eve, Noah, Moses, Jacob, King David, Jonah, Jonah's story about the big fish that caught him, Saint Peter's walk on the water. The whirlwind that took away the man and the chariot of fire. Daniel's story with the lions, those three Hebrew children in the fire. On and on goes those great stories, we shall all hear in person. Streets of gold, river of life, trees of life, throne of God. I hope everyone is as excited as I am for that wonderful day.

We were all blessed to make it through the COVID-19 virus, sad time. I know this is just the start of terrible times soon to come on. Important news: Jesus is still reaching out for us all to come to light. Hurry, while there is still the light, once the Holy Ghost is going, who knows if you can make Heaven. I pray these big preachers do move fast, I've warned them, time is about finished, they are waiting on a sign, just like all these men and women foolishly waited for. Noah, they waited till it was too late. King Agrippa laughed at Apostle Paul's words, they mocked Jesus, show us a sign. If you know the sun comes up in the morning, the moon comes out at night. Signs are all around us now, works everywhere, knowledge has increased in these far off days, what signs do you want? God has warned us, be ready for you know not the time or hour. Twinkle of the eye, so be truly ready for those trumpets to sound. Listen to those apostolic preachers, Acts 2:38-42 true salvation (words).

Amen and amen.

Chapter 10 Questions – Yes or No

1.(A) Did those apostles baptize in Jesus's name? Yes or No
(B) Were you baptized in Jesus's name? Yes or No
2.(A) Did they help others to receive the Holy Ghost? Yes or No
(B) Were about 3,000 souls added to church? Yes or No
3.(A) Did they say it was for all? Yes or No
(B) Did they preach and get others to obey? Acts 2:38 Yes or No
4.(A) Did they rebaptize others into Jesus's name? Yes or No
(B) Was the Holy Ghost, speaking in tongues still going on? Yes or No
5.(A) Was Simon saved after being baptized in Jesus's name? Yes or No
(B) Did Simon receive the Holy Ghost? Yes or No
6.(A) Did King Agrippa get saved by believing? Acts 26-28 Yes or No
(B) Did Paul wish others hearing to obey? Yes or No

7.(A) Do apostle's doctrine churches today still exist? Yes or No

(B) Will you preach and teach apostle's doctrine? Yes or No

8.(A) Do you believe God is still calling His church? Yes or No

(B) Do you know you're saved, like Jesus's first church? Yes or No

9.(A) Do you believe you have to work out your own salvation? Yes or No

(B) In James 2:17-20 does faith alone save you? Yes or No

10.(A) In Revelation 21:14 was Apostle Peter's name there? Yes or No

(B) Will you be like Apostle Paul, Lord what will thou have me to do? Acts 9:6,17,18 Yes or No

Final Warning

OT

Genesis 2:17 Adam was warned of death.

Genesis 4:6,7 Cain was warned.

Genesis 6:13 Noah was warned of flood. 12:1 Abram warned to leave the country. 19:26 Lot's wife looked back after being warned, turned into a pillar of salt.

Exodus 12:22 Moses warned to strike blood on the door for death to pass by.

II Kings 5:10-14 Man warned to dip 7 times to be made clean.

Proverbs 3:5 Trust in the Lord with all thine heart; and loan not unto thine own understanding.

Isaiah 55:6 Seek ye the Lord while he may be found, call ye upon him while he is near.

Joel 2:28,29 I will pour out my Spirit in the last days.

Jonah 1:1-17 Jonah was warned to go to Nineveh to preach. Big fish story.

Malachi 4:5 Warned all about the Lord coming.

NT

Matthew 1:20 Angel warned of Jesus's birth. 6:33 But seek ye first the Kingdom of God, and his righteousness; and all these things shall be added. 7:1 Judge not, that ye be not judged. 15:9 But in vain they do worship me, teaching for doctrines the commandments of men. 24:11 And many false prophets shall rise, and shall deceive many. 24:14 And this gospel of the Kingdom shall be preached in all the world for a witness unto all nations; and then shall the end come. 15 When ye therefore shall se the abomination of desolation, spoken by the prophet Daniel, stand in the holy place, (whosoever readeth, let him understand). 21 For then shall be great tribulation, such as was not since the beginning of the world to this time, no, nor ever shall be.

Mark 16:15 And he said unto them, go into (all) the world, and preach the gospel to every creature. 16 He that believeth and is (baptized) shall be saved; but he that believeth not shall be damned. 17 And these signs shall follow them that believe; in my name shall they cast out devils; they shall speak with new tongues.

John 3:5 Jesus answered, verily, verily, I say unto thee, except a man be (born of water and of the Spirit), he cannot enter into the Kingdom of God.

Acts 1:4 And being assembled together with them, commanded them that they should not depart from Jerusalem, but wait for the promise of the Father, which saith he, ye have heard of me. 5 For John truly baptized with water; but ye shall be baptized with the Holy Ghost not many days hence. 2:1-4 And they were all filled with the Holy Ghost and began to speak with other tongues, as the (Spirit) gave them utterance. 37-42 Now when they heard this, they were pricked in the heart, and said unto Peter and the rest of the apostles, men and brethren, what shall we do? 2:38 Then Peter said unto them, repent, and be baptized every one of you in the name of Jesus Christ for the remission of sins, and ye shall receive the gift of the Holy Ghost. 39 For the promise is unto you, and to your children, and to (all that afar off, even as many as the Lord our God shall call).

Acts 26:1-28 Apostle Paul explains the gospel, but King Agrippa said almost: Today millions almost become Christians, but the old tricky Devil fools them by false doctrine, took Jesus's name from baptism, speaking in tongues when you receive the Holy Ghost, let people believe it was just for the apostles, today they say raise your hand and believe you're saved, what a sad world because Jesus died and arose from the grave, those apostles and first true Christians were killed, hung on the cross, burnt to death, sawed to pieces, for (all) of us to the end of time.

It's time to build Jesus's church, we need apostles like Peter and Paul to preach and teach these lost souls, not the watered-down doctrine of man. God is about to destroy this sinful old world, He is ready to take us home. Those who sleep in Jesus, then those who are alive and remain in the air to those Saint Peter's pearly gates, we must help others to get truly born of water and the Spirit, just like Acts 2:38-42 the first church.

Warning to those big-name preachers, Pastor Joyce Myer, Pastor Franklin Graham, Pastor Joseph Prince, Pastor Creflo Dollar, Pastor Leon Fontaine, Pastor Bishop T.D. Jake, Pastor Robert Morris, Pastor Jentezen Franklin, all of you that received the Holy Ghost by speaking in tongues, you're hiding it under a bushel. Share your experience with others, Apostle Peter said in Acts 2:38-42 For the promise is for you, your children, and to (all) that are afar off, even as many as God shall call. 41 Then they that (gladly received) His word were baptized; and the same day there were added about three thousand souls. 42 And they continued steadfastly in the (apostle's doctrine).

Those apostles shared their Holy Ghost (Spirit) with 3,000 souls added, it wasn't just for them, it is for (all) to be born of water and Spirit. Jesus's church wasn't for a few. Apostle Peter and Apostle Paul died to reach out to (all) the world then and all afar off, you, your family, church members, to the whole, big world, time to get these souls truly saved.

Jesus wants to wash your sins away in His name (baptism) then fill all with the Holy Ghost (Spirit) by speaking in tongues, time to move is NOW. Final warning is for all His hungry sheep. Apostle Peter loved Jesus. Do you big preachers truly love Jesus? Feed his sheep, don't hide that (Spirit). Help (all) to get this wonderful gift of Holy Ghost. As we see the news, we know the time is winding down. Get ready, get ready, to those gates.

I pray to God that preachers reach their lost souls. If you miss the rapture of the saints and you're lucky enough to survive through the destruction of end-time war, I hope you will reach the lost souls left alive. Who knows God's time, but we all know it's closer than ever before. The knowledge has exploded like never before. Gospel has reached the whole world now.

Israel has become a nation, so many warning signs already, why take a chance? Tonight, tomorrow isn't promised to anyone. Jesus said be ready, for we know not the time nor the hour. Twinkle of an eye is fast, just like jets and trains, just like God took (Enoch) in Genesis 5:24 or in II Kings 2:11 (Elijah) in whirlwind into heaven, or like (Jesus) in Acts 1:9 He was taken up in a cloud, out of sight.

So, when Jesus breaks the sky, who shall know the second it shall be? As we all know, God is closer now than ever before to finish His plans. Who wants to hear depart from me, you work of iniquity? Oh, how sad.

Now preachers, God wants us all to stir up the gift of the Holy Ghost (Spirit). God is calling you all to finish His church, just like the first church. He is preparing us now to trample down those devils and demons' tricky work.

Apostles in these end far-off days, are you all ready to feed his sheep? I know humbleness and pride are hard to break but look at those apostles. God is no respecter of persons, He wants to use us today, just like then. Apostle Paul thought he was right, look how he finished his race for Jesus. Just think, one million years, just like a day for us in Heaven with Jesus.

Call those preachers, see how each of you truly are born of the Spirit. Know that God has placed you each in time to finish his church. Please don't just think you all received the gift of the (Spirit) to hide. It's time now to march those saints afar off towards Saint Peter's Gates. Stir up the gift now in Jesus's lovely name, get baptized in Jesus's lovely name. Now preach like those apostles, 3,000 souls added. How many today shall receive the true plan of salvation, amen?

Jesus is coming soon, could be morning, night, or noon. Oh, when the saints come marching in, when they crown Him King of Kings, let's all afar off be in that number. Are you ready? Do you truly want to feed Jesus's sheep? Get into the light, God is calling us all out of the darkness now. Let us finish our race like Apostle Peter and Apostle Paul, amen, amen.

Chapter 11

If God lets me write another book in my lifetime, I'll truly let you all know the battle that is coming soon. Who knows what God has for time to us all far off days. I have many books to write if God allows me to live, to finish these things, maybe just this book, who knows His ways.

This is His first big warning to get ready for the (taken away). But it may be the only warning I may give unto this world. Like I said, I'm starting the second book, and third is on my heart and mind, I pray I'll finish these books of far off times.

Don't wait on nothing, questions are in the apostolic churches to be answered. Acts 2:38-42 For us all, even to the end of time. All preachers can preach Apostle Peter's words, they know the scriptures well. I pray they will share the true Holy Ghost filling, speaking in tongues, laying on hands, baptizing into Jesus's name for the remission of your sins, as John 3:3-5 Water and the Spirit for to be born again ready for the Kingdom.

Search the scriptures, study them like never before. Awaken

from the darkness into the light (truth). Your eternal life, your loved ones, your family, your church's Brothers and Sisters, don't waste time, tomorrow isn't promised to anyone. I know Jesus died for us all, even like sinners as we all once was in those past times. Praise God for his truth, grace, and mercy.

Amen, Brothers and Sisters.

Walking In the Kingdom

OT

Genesis 5:24 And Enoch walked with God: and he was not; for God took him. 28:12 Jacob and he dreamed, and behold a ladder set up on the Earth, and the top reached to Heaven: and behold the angels of God ascending and descending on it. 13 And the Lord stood above it. 32:1 And Jacob went on his way, and the angels of God met him. 19:1 And there came two angels to Sodom at even; and Lot sat in the gate of Sodom; and Lot seeing them rose up to meet them; and he bowed himself with his face toward the ground; 2 And he said, behold now, my lords, turn in, I pray you, into your servant's house and tarry all night, and wash your feet.

II Kings 2:11 And it came to pass as they still went on and talked that behold, there appeared a chariot of fire, and horses of fire, and parted them both asunder; and Elijah went up by a whirlwind into Heaven.

Job 9:8 Which alone spreadeth out the heavens, and treadeth (walk) of sea.

Psalm 104:3 Who layeth the beams of his chambers in the waters; who maketh the clouds his chariots who walketh upon the wings of the wind.

Daniel 3:25 He answered and said, lo, I see four men loose, walking in the midst of fire, and they were not hurt; and the form of the fourth is like the son of God. 6:22 My God hath sent his angel, and hath shut the lion's mouths that they have not hurt me. 10:13 Then said he unto me, fear not, Daniel; for from the first day that thou didest set thine heart to understand and to chasten thyself before thy God, thy words were heard, and I am come for thy words. 13 But the prince of the kingdom of Persia withstood me one and twenty days; but lo, Michael, one of the chief princes came to help me; and I remained there with the kings of Persia.

Zechariah 6:5 And the angel answered and said unto me, these are the four spirits of the heavens, which go forth standing before the Lord of all the Earth.

NT

3:1,2 And saying repent ye, for the Kingdom of Heaven is at hand. John's words. 4:17 From that time Jesus began to preach and to say repent, for the Kingdom of Heaven is at hand.

Luke 11:18 If Satan also be divided against himself, how shall (his kingdom) stand? Because ye say that I cast out devils through Beelzebub. 19 And if by Beelzebub cast out devils, by whom do your sons cast them out? Therefore, shall they be your judges. 20 But if I with the finger of God cast out devils, no doubt the Kingdom of God is come upon you.

Luke 9:27-34 Transfiguration. But I tell you of a truth, there be some standing here which shall not taste of death till they see the Kingdom of God. 28 And it came to pass about 8 days after these sayings, he took Peter and John and James, and went up into a mountain to pray. 29 And as he prayed, the fashion of his countenance was altered, and his raiment was white and glistening. 30 And behold, there talked with him two men, which was Moses and Elias. 31 Who appeared in glory and spoke of his decease which he should accomplish at Jerusalem. 20:38 For he is not a God of the dead, but of the living; for all live unto him.

John 11:25 Jesus said unto her, I am the resurrection and the life; he that believeth in me, though he were dead, yet shall he live. 26 And whosoever liveth and believeth in me shall never die, believest thou this? 43 And when he thus had spoken, he cried with a loud voice, Lazarus, come forth. 44 And he that was dead came forth.

Acts 5:19 But the angel of the Lord by night opened the prison doors and brought them forth, and said; 20 Go, stand and speak in the temple to the people all the words of life.

Acts 9:3 And as he journeyed, he came near Damascus: and suddenly there shined round about him a light from Heaven. 4 And he fell to the Earth and heard a voice saying unto him, Saul, Saul, why persecutest thou me? 5 And he said, who art thou, Lord? And the Lord said, I am Jesus whom thou persecutest. It is hard for thee to kick against the prick. 26:18 To open their eyes and turn them from darkness to light, and from the power of Satan unto God that they may receive forgiveness of sins and inheritance among them which are sanctified by faith that is in me.

I Corinthians 4:20 For the Kingdom of God is not in word, but in power. 15:24 Then cometh the end, when he shall have delivered up the kingdom to God, even the Father; when he shall have put down all rule and all authority and power.

II Corinthians 12:2 I knew a man in Christ above fourteen

years ago (whether in the body or out, I can not tell; God knoweth), such a one caught up to the third heaven. 4 Into paradise.

John 3: Jesus answered and said unto him, verily, verily, I say unto thee, except a man be born (again), he cannot see the Kingdom of God. 6 That which is born of the flesh is flesh; and that which is born of the (Spirit) is Spirit. Now Jesus is calling us all to be born again.

Acts 2:38-42 Spirit given to those gladly received the promise, most people today reject the true Spirit filling. They think it was for those first early holy rollers, but Peter said for us all and afar off. End time saints of God, oh how blessed we are to receive the same Spirit.

I still think about it today, October 1, right on my oldest son's birthday, I was baptized in Jesus's lovely name, but I didn't receive the Holy Spirit. I saw others coming out of the water, speaking in tongues, about 15 others, but I didn't receive my gift of speaking in tongues until about two weeks later, then I was so glad, I knew I was born again of the water and Spirit, praise God for his grace and mercy.

Then I knew that God was no respecter of person if he gave the (Spirit) to some sinner like I once was, that he would give the Holy Ghost to anyone that asked in faith. The first time I spoke in other tongues, it scared (frightened) me. It felt like a doctor or dentist started to move my tongue and words (strange words) came out of my mouth. I was startled a lot, but after that day I understood the Holy Ghost could come on you any time of worship or praying. I sometimes speak for minutes, sometimes for hours, who knows the Spirit's plans in you except the Spirit? Most times it sounds different, once or twice I spoke in China or Japan tongues, I never know what language.

OT

Genesis 11:7 Go to, let us go down, and there confound their language that they may not understand one another's speech. Too much for that time, knowledge too fast in time.

Daniel 12:4 But though, O Daniel, shut up the words and seal this book, even to the time of the end; many shall run to and fro, and knowledge shall be increased.

NT

Now in Acts 2:4 And they were all filled with the Holy Ghost and began to speak with other tongues, as the Spirit gave them utterance. So now we see that God can change language or tongues when he wants to confound a man, the Spirit was poured out in pentecost day, early first church, just like Joel 2:28,29.

I Corinthians 2:10 But God has revealed them unto us by his (Spirit) for the (Spirit) searchest all things, yeah, the deep things of God.

Galatians 5:25 If we live in the (Spirit), let us also walk in the Spirit.

Ephesians 5:14 Wherefore he saith, awake from the dead (sleep) and Christ shall give thee (light).

Philippians 2:5 Let this mind be in you, which was also in Christ Jesus.

I Timothy 4:13-16 Till I come, give attendance to reading, to exhortation, to doctrine. 14 Neglect not the gift (Holy Ghost) that is in thee, which was given thee by prophecy with the laying on the hands of presbytery (of a church) first church.

Acts 19:6 (Paul)

I Timothy 4:15 Meditate upon these things; give thyself wholly to them; that thy propheting may appear to all. 16 Take heed unto thyself; and to the (doctrine); continue in them; for in doing this thou shalt save thyself, and them that hear thee.

II Timothy 2:15 Study to show thyself approved unto God, a workman that needeth not be ashamed, rightly dividing the truth.

I Corinthians 15:22 For as in Adam all die, even so in Christ shall all be made alive.

Acts 2:38 Then Peter said unto them, (repent) and be baptized every one of you in the name of (Jesus Christ) for the (remission of sins) and ye shall receive the gift of the Holy Ghost (Spirit). 41 Then they that (gladly) received His word were (baptized): and the same day there were added unto them about 3,000 souls. 42 And they continued steadfastly in the (apostle's doctrine) and fellowship.

John 3:5 Except a man be born of water of the (Spirit) he cannot enter into the Kingdom of God. 6 That which is flesh born is flesh, and that which is born of the (Spirit) is Spirit.

John 4:24 God is a Spirit, and they that worship him most worship him in Spirit and truth. 5:39,40 Search the scriptures; for in them ye (think) ye have eternal life, and they are they which testify of me. 40 And ye will not come to me that ye might have life.

Acts 10:34 Then Peter opened his mouth and said, of a truth I perceive that God is no respecter of persons. 42 And he commanded us to preach unto the people and to testify that it is he which was ordained of God to be the judge of quick and dead. 43 To him gave all the prophets witness, that through His name whosoever believeth in Him shall receive remission of sins. 44 While Peter yet spoke these words, the Holy Ghost fell on all them which heard the word. 45 And they of the circumcision which believed were astonished, as many as came with Peter because that on the Gentiles also was poured out the gift of the Holy Ghost. 46 For they heard them (speak with tongues) and magnify God. Then answered Peter; 47 Can any man forbid water that these should not be baptized which have received the Holy Ghost as well as we? 48 Then he commanded them to be baptized in the (name) of the Lord.

John 3:3-5 Yes?

Romans 8:6-13 11 But if the (Spirit) of him that raised up Jesus from the dead dwelleth in you, he that raised up Christ from the dead shall also quicken your mortal bodies by his (Spirit) that dwelleth in you. Quicken (alive), the (quick to lose), to (lose from the dead), give life (rouse), bring out of sleep, stir up, wake up, awake from dead. Adam brought (death) being dead, the death of our hope (promise) eternal life, we all are dead till the (Spirit) quickens us into eternal life, God-like, saint, heavenly, pure.

Acts 26:18 To open their eyes and to turn them from darkness (dark), lacking information, ignorant, hidden, secret, my light, lack of knowledge, fact, understanding, unwise, to the light, and from the power of Satan unto God that they may receive forgiveness of sins and inheritance (birth right).

John 3:3-8 5 Except go be born of water and (Spirit). We are (all) born in flesh, we must be born again of water and Spirit.

Acts 2:38 Jesus's name

Philippians 2:5 Let this mind be in you which was also in Christ Jesus. 12 Work out your own salvation with fear and trembling. Eternal life is there for all that obey. Apostle Peter is giving keys to all who gladly receive his words. Apostle Paul obeyed Jesus's words. He died to bring the true gospel to us all, even (us) a far-off end times. God's plan of salvation, we all must choose, life or stay in darkness, death. Satan truly wants all to stay in darkness. God is bringing light to us, life forever. You alone must choose, your family, your church, your friends must come to light, life. King Agrippa chose darkness, all his family and friends followed his choice, sadly. Today if you hear his voice, harden not your heart, tomorrow isn't promised. Master is calling today, come to his saving light, come out of the darkness.

Revelation 21:1-27 27 Lamb's book of life is your name written there? Amen, amen.

Conclusion

You can come out of the darkness into the (quicken) light. God has given us the prophets, Moses, apostles, and Jesus laid down His life for us all, from Adam to the far off final day of time.

Old Testament, New Testament, apostlic, apostle's doctrine, same for about 2,000 years now, so you have a view of the light. If you like darkness, God will not force you to the (light). Saint Peter's Gate is wide open for you, and you only must make the final choice, obey God's plan or Hellfire.

Well, my preacher doesn't believe it's for us today, then Saint Peter didn't get that preacher isn't bound in Heaven.

Matthew 16:19 Those preachers will not be standing at the throne of God with you. You have to work out your own salvation with fear and trembling.

Philippians 2:12 Apostle Paul learned that himself. The old Devil laughs at us when we say, well I believe a preacher. Those preachers, sadly, are blind of the darkness of deceitful devils. He tricked Adam and Eve, so how easily can he trick the world?

Kill, steal, destroy. Jesus came to this world to show us the light (quicken) us all from out of the darkness into light, eternal life.

Who will listen to Saint Peter's words (keys) to the Kingdom? Jesus is calling his sheep, hear the master's voice, awaken from the dead, come to the light of the world, as Acts 2:38-42.

Luke 11:13 God wants us (all) to receive the Holy Ghost.

Acts 2:39.

John 3:3-5 Born of water and Spirit.

I Corinthians 2:10 But God has revealed them unto us by his Spirit; for the Spirit searchest (all) things, yeah, the (deep things) of God.

II Corinthians 13:5 Examine yourselves, whether ye be in the (faith); prove your own selves, know ye not your own selves; how that Jesus Christ is in you, except ye be reprobates?

Romans 8:10 And if Christ be in you, the body is dead because of sin; but the (Spirit) is (quicken) life because of righteousness.

(?) Question? Are you (Jesus)? Are you (quicken) in the Spirit? You are darkness or light. Adam all die (darkness). Jesus all (life). Spirit.

Amen and amen.

I hope you read and understood this book. If you have any questions on your (faith) call an apostolic church. There are a few in every town or city. Don't leave your (eternal life) in someone's hands. It is too (precious), too important to lose. Oh, how sadly people are lost forever because they didn't search the (scriptures) rightly dividing the word of truth.

II Timothy 2:13 Dear Brothers and Sisters, Heaven, please don't miss the rapture day. If some do miss that day, I hope and pray they can still find the way there if they make it through the seven-year tribulation. Who knows the hard times that shall take the world then?

I praise God for His grace and mercy on my once lost soul. Jesus broke those chains of Hell and death from my future. I still can't understand because I know Hell I deserved. Praise God for his cross and forgiveness. I wish others could believe and forgive like our loving Father. He deserves all crowns, I say all crowns, not just one crown, all our crowns in Heaven.

If you feel like writing a letter, don't thank me for this book, thank and praise God for all His grace and mercy He gives. I'm on my way of the second book, the Holy Ghost has given me the next title already, share with family, church, and friends.

By Clark Smith #273-624
W.C.I.
13800 McMullen-High Way
Cumberland, Maryland 21502

ABOUT THE AUTHOR

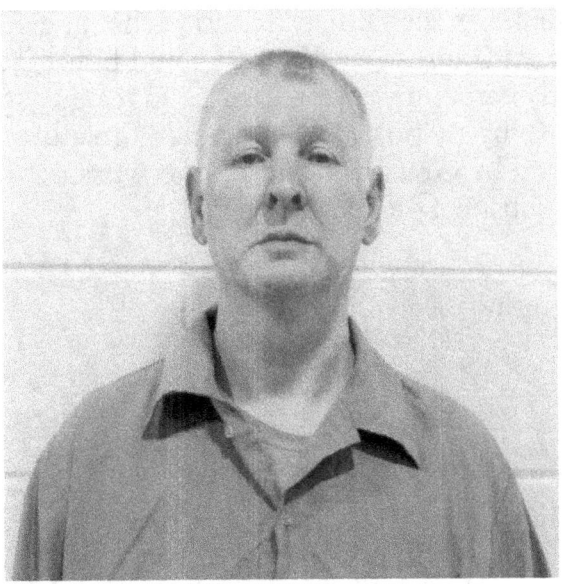

I'm an Apostolic Born-Again Brother in Christ Jesus. I follow the Apostles doctrine, that was told in ACTS 2:38-42. In John 3:3-5, Jesus said all must be born of water and Spirit. In this book, you will understand the True Doctrine Salvation. If you have any questions, call or go to the nearest Apostolic Church. As you search the Bible, pray the Holy Ghosts opens your heart. I take no credit for this book, Holy Ghost wants All to understand. I'm just a born-again, true brother, trying to guide men and women into Saint Peter's Gates, all must follow those first 120 Saints.

Jesus is calling his sheep. Who will follow his voice?

Saint Peter was given the keys, ACTS book shows the way. Apostle Paul was showing others in ACTS 19:1-6. He re-baptized those in Jesus' lovely name, helped them receive the speaking in tongues, if you follow the Apostles ways, you shall enter those gates.

I only wrote what those Apostles, already written 2,000 years ago. As a true brother in Christ Jesus, I'm doing Jesus' true doctrine. The LORD is my shepherd, I heard his voice, Jesus is calling. I'm just a man that loves helping All to Eternal Life with Jesus. We all must stand before Jesus, do you want His name in your baptism, and tongue speaking, just like those first Apostolic Saints did? I'm a brother that was saved by Grace and Mercy. No work of my own, Apostles Doctrine True Salvation Way,

From Brother,

Clarke Smith

www.ingramcontent.com/pod-product-compliance
Lightning Source LLC
Chambersburg PA
CBHW071910070526
44583CB00016B/1928